FRESHWATER FISHING

BY S.L. HAMILTON

A&D Xtreme
An Imprint of Abdo Publishing | www.abdopublishing.com

Visit us at
www.abdopublishing.com

Published by Abdo Publishing Company, a division of ABDO, PO Box 398166, Minneapolis, Minnesota 55439. Copyright ©2015 by Abdo Consulting Group, Inc. International copyrights reserved in all countries. No part of this book may be reproduced in any form without written permission from the publisher. A&D Xtreme™ is a trademark and logo of Abdo Publishing Company.

Printed in the United States of America, North Mankato, Minnesota.
102014
012015

 PRINTED ON RECYCLED PAPER

Editor: John Hamilton
Graphic Design: Sue Hamilton
Cover Design: Sue Hamilton
Cover Photo: Alamy
Interior Photos: Alamy-pgs 12-13, 22-23, 26 & 27; AlaskaStock-pg 28; Corbis-pgs 21 & 29; Glow Images-pg 9; Humminbird-pg 9 (inset); iStock-pgs 1, 6-7, 8, 10 & 30 (inset); James Smedley-pgs 4-5, 11, 14-15, 16-17, 18-19 & 20; Nicholas Ebinger-pgs 2-3, 24-25 & 31; Rapala USA-pg 31 (inset); ThinkStock-pgs 30-31.

Websites
To learn more about Fishing, visit booklinks.abdopublishing.com. These links are routinely monitored and updated to provide the most current information available.

Library of Congress Control Number: 2014944876

Cataloging-in-Publication Data

Hamilton, S.L.
 Freshwater fishing / S.L. Hamilton.
   p. cm. -- (Xtreme fishing)
ISBN 978-1-62403-681-1 (lib. bdg.)
Includes index.
1. Fishing--Juvenile literature. 2. Freshwater fishes--Juvenile literature. I. Title.
799.1/1--dc23

                              2014944876

Contents

Freshwater Fishing 4

Rods & Reels 6

Tackle 8

Bass 10

Trout 12

Walleye 14

Northern Pike. .16

Muskellunge 18

Salmon 20

Channel Catfish 22

Sunfish 24

Crappies 26

Perch. 27

Dangers 28

Glossary. 30

Index 32

Freshwater Fishing

Freshwater fishing pits anglers against game fish in local lakes, rivers, and streams. Some of the most delicious fish are found close to home. They are as clever as they are tasty.

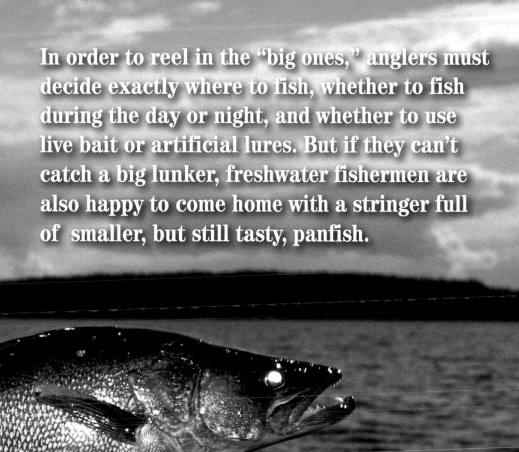

In order to reel in the "big ones," anglers must decide exactly where to fish, whether to fish during the day or night, and whether to use live bait or artificial lures. But if they can't catch a big lunker, freshwater fishermen are also happy to come home with a stringer full of smaller, but still tasty, panfish.

Rods & Reels

Freshwater fishing rods and reels range from very simple to high tech. Fishing rods are usually made of graphite, fiberglass, or bamboo. They are designed to bend, but not break. Spinning and casting rods, and their matching reels, are often used for freshwater fishing.

Spinning and casting reels allow anglers to cast their lines at a distance and with great accuracy.

XTREME FACT– Fishing rods may cost anywhere from $25 to nearly $4,000. Fishing reels may cost from $25 up to $1,300.

Tackle

The tackle, or gear, needed by freshwater fishermen includes such things as a tackle box of lures, fishing line, extra hooks, as well as a net and a stringer or basket for their catch. Many anglers fish with live bait. A bait bucket of minnows or a container of worms or leeches is kept close at hand.

Some anglers fish on or near the shoreline. Waders and good boots keep feet dry. Hats and vests protect against the elements, as well as provide pockets to carry equipment. Many people fish from boats. Some boats are equipped with electronic fishfinders.

XTREME FACT – Some fishfinders locate fish and sound an alarm to alert the angler.

Bass

Largemouth and smallmouth bass are sought by many anglers. Largemouth bass may reach up to 20 pounds (9 kg). They strike on artificial lures or live bait. They are found in freshwater where there are plenty of submerged weeds, logs, or brush.

XTREME FACT– When hooked, largemouth bass will rush to the surface, open their mouths, and shake their heads in an attempt to throw the hook. They also sometimes dive down and wrap the fishing line around submerged obstacles.

Smallmouth bass grow to 12 pounds (5 kg) and are known for their fighting stamina and leaping ability. They will bite on smaller lures or bait. Some anglers consider smallmouth bass the sportiest freshwater fish.

Trout

Rainbow, brook, brown, golden, cutthroat, lake, bull, and Dolly Varden trout are fun to catch and delicious to eat. Trout range in size from about 1 to 8 pounds (.5 - 3.6 kg). Trout are fighters. Rainbows are known to leap out of the water several times before they are landed. Trout bite on artificial lures and flies, as well as live bait such as leeches and minnows.

XTREME FACT– Rainbow trout have been caught using mini-marshmallows as bait.

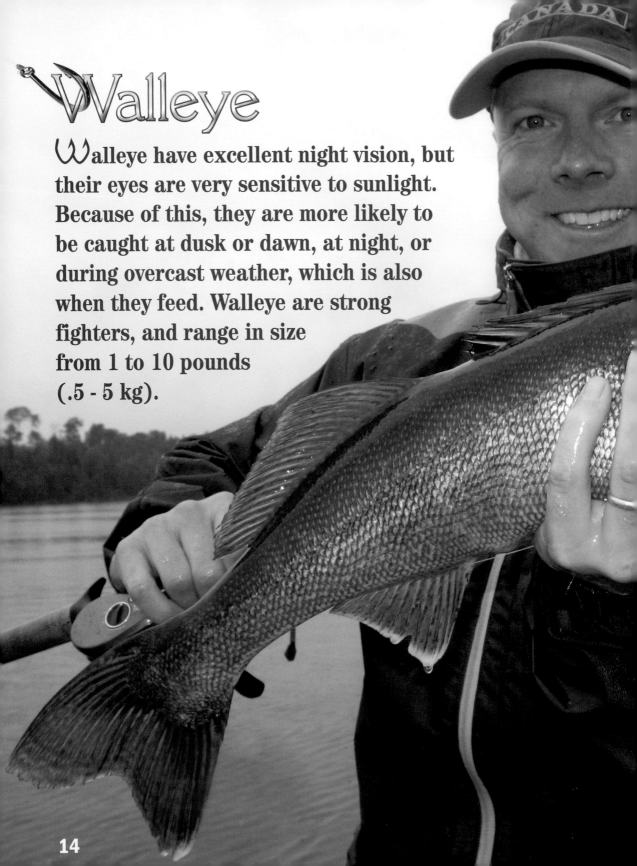

Walleye

Walleye have excellent night vision, but their eyes are very sensitive to sunlight. Because of this, they are more likely to be caught at dusk or dawn, at night, or during overcast weather, which is also when they feed. Walleye are strong fighters, and range in size from 1 to 10 pounds (.5 - 5 kg).

14

Walleye reside in clean, hard-bottomed lakes and streams. They prefer areas where they can go from light to dark quickly, often hiding near rocks. In the summer, they retreat to deeper waters where the temperature is cooler. Walleye are often said to be the best tasting of any freshwater fish.

XTREME FACT– Walleye are nicknamed marble eyes and glass eyes.

Northern Pike

Northern pike are fierce fish with a mouthful of sharp teeth. They grow big, with weights ranging from 6 to 24 pounds (3 to 11 kg). Northern pike eat fish, but also frogs, crayfish, mice, muskrats, and ducklings. They will bite on just about anything that looks like lunch to them, which makes northerns easier to catch than other game fish.

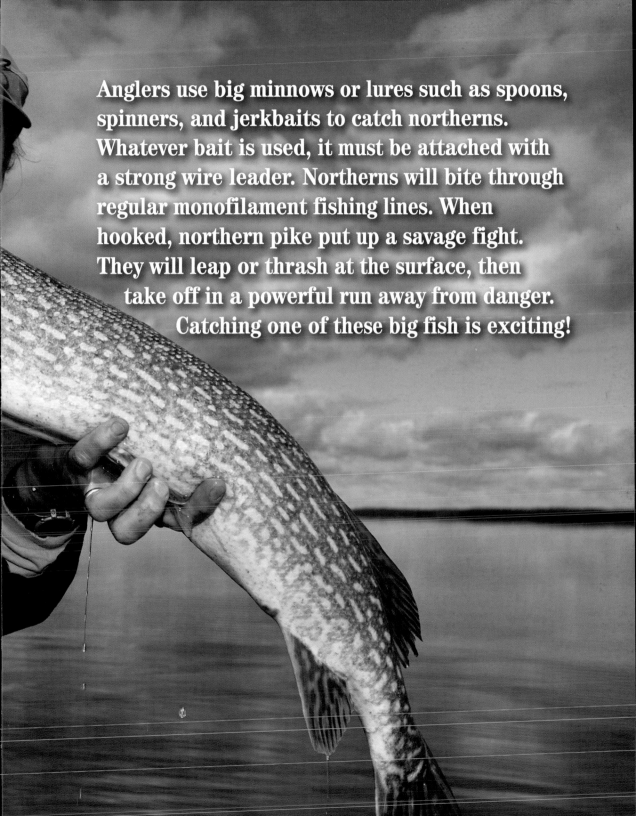

Anglers use big minnows or lures such as spoons, spinners, and jerkbaits to catch northerns. Whatever bait is used, it must be attached with a strong wire leader. Northerns will bite through regular monofilament fishing lines. When hooked, northern pike put up a savage fight. They will leap or thrash at the surface, then take off in a powerful run away from danger. Catching one of these big fish is exciting!

Muskellunge

Muskellunge, or muskies, are found in lakes in the northeastern United States. Sometimes confused with northern pike, their coloring is lighter, but their nature is just as fierce. Also, muskies are bigger. They range in size from 6 to 46 pounds (3 - 21 kg).

Muskies prefer warmer waters. They lurk among the weeds of shallow lakes or slow-moving rivers. Big muskies go for big bait. They hit on long plugs and spinners, or baitfish weighing up to 1 pound (.5 kg). Once hooked, muskies put up a short but fierce battle. They are known to make swift underwater runs that may break the fishing line or even straighten the hook, allowing them to escape.

Salmon

Chinook salmon may grow up to 43 pounds (20 kg). They are caught using erratic-action spoons and flies, salmon egg-baited spinners, or pieces of baitfish. Chinook are known to make runs that take 200 to 300 yards (183 to 274 m) of line and then dive down deeply. Chinook will fight for half an hour.

Coho salmon reach an average weight of 5 to 10 pounds (2 to 5 kg). Coho live near the water's surface. They bite on spoons, spinners, plugs, and flies. Coho are fun to catch. These acrobatic fish will leap and switch directions so fast that anglers are often fooled into thinking they've thrown the hook.

XTREME FACT– *Chinook and coho salmon are anadromous, meaning they are born and spawn in freshwater, but live their lives in saltwater.*

Channel Catfish

Channel catfish are bottom-dwellers. Their whiskers, or "barbels," are used to locate food at the bottom of rivers, lakes, and ponds throughout the central and eastern United States. They range in size from 3 to 20 pounds (1 to 9 kg).

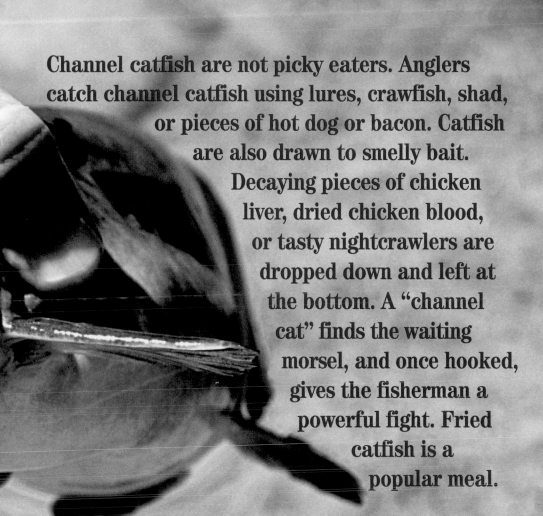

Channel catfish are not picky eaters. Anglers catch channel catfish using lures, crawfish, shad, or pieces of hot dog or bacon. Catfish are also drawn to smelly bait. Decaying pieces of chicken liver, dried chicken blood, or tasty nightcrawlers are dropped down and left at the bottom. A "channel cat" finds the waiting morsel, and once hooked, gives the fisherman a powerful fight. Fried catfish is a popular meal.

XTREME FACT– Catfish are often caught using bait soap. This soft, non-crumbling soap is filled with tasty fish-attracting bait bits. It is packed on a hook, and catfish love it. Some catfish anglers have their own family recipe for this special soap.

Sunfish

Several species of sunfish are found throughout the United States, southern Canada, and northern Mexico. Although small, ranging in size from .25 to 1 pound (.1 to .5 kg), they are tough fighters for their size. Sunfish go after live bait such as worms, leeches, tiny minnows, crickets, grasshoppers, and grubs. Small poppers, dry flies, tiny jigs and spinners are also used. They are tasty fish and fun to catch.

XTREME FACT– One species of sunfish are called bluegills. When hooked, these fish will flip onto their sides and swim in circles, pulling as hard as fish twice their size.

Crappies

Black and white crappies are found in lakes and slow-moving rivers throughout much of the United States. These small panfish reach sizes of .5 to 2 pounds (.2 to .9 kg). They will bite on small flies, minnows, and insect larvae. Anglers also catch crappies with small flies, spinners, jigs, and crankbaits. Black crappies are stronger fighters than white crappies. They are both good eating.

Perch

Perch are considered one of the most delicious freshwater fish. They are found mainly in the northern United States and Canada. They range in size from .25 to 1.2 pounds (.1 to .5 kg). Bigger perch are located in large lakes. They are easy to catch. Daytime feeders, they will bite on small minnows, worms, leeches, crickets, grubs, and crayfish tails. Small jigs and spinners are also used.

Dangers

Freshwater anglers need to be careful in remote areas where they may encounter wildlife. Bears, deer, moose, and wolves live near lakes, rivers, and streams. It's important to be aware of one's surroundings and be prepared to leave or defend oneself if necessary.

No matter how experienced the angler, getting impaled by a fishhook is always possible. If left uncleaned and untreated, hook injuries can resul in infections. If a person gets hooked, it's a good idea to leave in the hook and go directly to a medical facility. A doctor can remove the hook, then clean and treat the injured area. To avoid getting "hooked," anglers must stay focused when casting, attaching lures or bait, and unhooking fish.

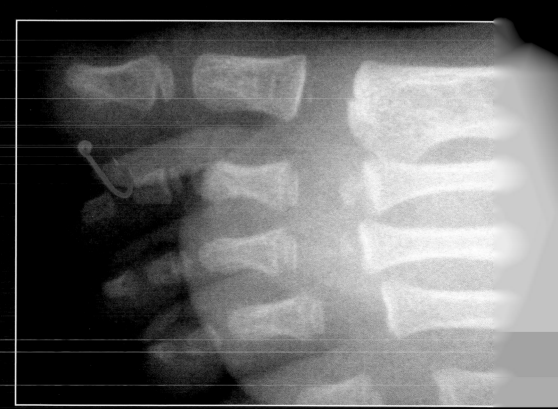

An x-ray shows a foot with a fishhook in one of the toes.

Glossary

ANADROMOUS
Fish that spend much of their lives in saltwater, but swim up freshwater rivers to spawn. Chinook and coho salmon are anadromous.

BAITFISH
Smaller fish on which game fish regularly feed.

BARBELS
Whisker-like organs found near the mouths of certain fish such as catfish. The barbels act as taste buds.

CRANKBAIT
A lure that resembles a minnow with a lip or bill in front whose size and angle determine how deep the lure will go in the water.

FIBERGLASS
A reinforced plastic material, fiberglass is made of glass fibers embedded in a resin. Fishing rods made of fiberglass are flexible and tough, but may be heavier than rods made of other materials, such as graphite.

FISH FINDER
An electronic device that sends out sound waves under water. The sound waves bounce back and present a picture

of such things as fish, weeds, rocks, and the depth of the water in a certain area.

GRAPHITE
A material used to make lighter-yet-stronger, more-sensitive fishing rods.

JERKBAIT
Soft- or hard-plastic lures that look like baitfish. Anglers cast and retrieve the lures using a series of quick jerks. This makes the lures look like darting fish.

LARVAE
The worm-like form of many insects when they are newly hatched, prior to changing into their winged, adult shape. Fish feed on insect larvae.

LUNKER
A very large fish relative to its species.

MONOFILAMENT
A clear, flexible nylon filament used in fishing lines. Monofilaments are available in many strengths.

Index

A
anadromous 21

B
bait soap 23
baitfish 19, 20
bamboo 6
barbels 22
bass 10
black crappie 26
bluegill 25
brook trout 12
brown trout 12
bull trout 12

C
Canada 24, 27
casting reel 7
casting rod 6
catfish 22, 23
channel catfish 22, 23
chinook salmon 20, 21
coho salmon 21
crankbait 26
crappies 26
cutthroat
   trout 12

D
Dolly Varden trout 12

F
fiberglass 6
fish finder 9

G
golden trout 12
graphite 6

J
jerkbait 17

L
lake trout 12
largemouth bass 10
larvae 26
lunker 5

M
Mexico 24
monofilament 17
muskellunge 18
muskie 18, 19

N
northern pike 16, 17, 18

P
panfish 5, 26
perch 27

R
rainbow trout 12

S
salmon 20, 21
smallmouth bass 10, 11
spinning reel 6
spinning rod 6
stringer 5, 8
sunfish 24, 25

T
tackle 8
tackle box 8
trout 12

U
United States 18, 22, 24, 27

W
waders 9
walleye 14, 15
white crappie 26